Sales

Easily Sell Anything To

Anyone & Achieve Sales

Excellence In 7 Simple Steps

Steve Gold

Introduction

To the uninitiated or the novice, the art of selling may feel like a mystical process that only a select few people are able to grasp. The truth, however, is far from that simple. Selling is in fact a skill that can be learned. Although it does take time to master, it is more than accessible to anyone willing to commit themselves to the art.

You may be wondering then, what makes a successful salesperson and how can one hope to achieve that level of expertise? Are there specific tactics, teachings and a proverbial "bag of tricks" that one can memorize and employ to begin raking in large profits from their sales activities? The quick answer to this is, I'm afraid, no. Sales cannot be simplified to this extent, which in one way is a positive thing, otherwise every businesses would have no problem turning over profits and flourishing the moment they open up their doors. This, of course is unrealistic and would be unsustainable as the market dictates that some businesses must fail while others flourish.

When you work in sales, you are essentially dealing with people's demands. To put it simply, successful sales people need to understand their target market's wants and needs. This knowledge must be coupled with the ability to convince potential customers – through various marketing means and channels – that your products and services can provide them with the solutions they have been looking for. Not only that, you also need to convince them that you are offering a product that is better than is being offered by competing businesses. When put like this it sounds fairly simple, but the truth is, the sales process is far from straight forward.

As a salesperson, your job has many layers. First, you need to tout the best features and perks of whatever it is that you are offering your customers. Next, you have to demonstrate – as convincingly as you can – how buying from you will help the customer with whatever they problem they need to solve. Even after all the hard work has been implemented in the sales process, you may still even end up with a 'no' from the customer. Indeed, part of a salesperson's job is also to learn to deal with rejections. After all, the popular analogy that a good salesperson can sell ice to

Eskimos is nothing more than a myth. No one can sell to anyone, but a good salesperson can sell to those who need the things he or she has to offer.

An important thing to understand is that a good sales track record is more than just meeting the targeted profit margin. It also has a lot to do with building lasting business relationship with customers based on trust, as there is nothing more valuable to a business than customer loyalty.

Whether sales is your livelihood, or you are an entrepreneur looking to market your goods and services to customers, this book contained little doses of wisdom on succeeding in sales – from selling, building customer rapport, tried-and-true tricks of the trade, and even how to handle rejection. All these information are organized in a direct and concise manner for your light reading pleasure.

Before you delve any deeper into the art of selling, though, let us not forget the two most crucial, yet rarely mentioned components of successful sales: patience and perseverance. Cultivate whose traits as you improve your selling game, good luck and happy selling!

FREE BONUS!

As a free bonus, I've included a preview of one of my other best-selling books, "Elon Musk - The Biography of a Modern Day Renaissance Man"at the end of this book!

ALSO...

Be sure to check out my other books. Scroll to the back of this book for a list of other books written by me, Steve Gold!

This document is geared towards providing exact and reliable information in regards to the topic and issue covered. The publication is sold with the idea that the publisher is not required to render accounting, officially permitted, or otherwise, qualified services. If advice is necessary, legal or professional, a practiced individual in the profession should be ordered.

- From a Declaration of Principles which was accepted and approved equally by a Committee of the American Bar Association and a Committee of Publishers and Associations.

The information provided herein is stated to be truthful and consistent, in that any liability, in terms of inattention or otherwise, by any usage or abuse of any policies, processes, or directions contained within is the solitary and utter responsibility of the recipient reader. Under no circumstances will any legal responsibility or blame be held against the publisher

Table of contents

Chapter 1

Know Your Products & Services

Familiarize yourself with what you

are selling!

The reason for losing a customer can be baffling for an inexperience salesperson, especially when they've come so close to making the sale. How could it have happened when the quality of the products and services speak for themselves? After all, a co-worker selling the same stuff is able to rake in countless sales. Is there a "secret" trick-of-the-trade that is somehow inaccessible to you?

The answers to your sales woes may simply be a lack of thorough product knowledge. The importance of knowing what you are selling inside-out can not be stressed enough. A true salesperson should not only know what they are selling, but also know how to make customers see and understand all the benefits that their product or service has to offer. Simply put, sales can be considered as a branch of "the art of persuasion".

It is vitally important to have in-depth knowledge of one's products and services.

Knowledgeable salespeople are able to give a more convincing sales pitch and handle customers' objections. They cater to customers' needs and convince potential buyers that the right solutions can be found in the products and services they are selling. If a salesperson does not possess the required product knowledge, even the best product in the world will remain on the shelf, resulting in the loss of potential profit.

Furthermore, product knowledge can help boost a salesperson's confidence when handling customers objections to making a purchase. Having solid product knowledge shows that the salesperson knows exactly what he or she is talking about. This makes them better at offering assistance and presenting solutions – in the form of their products and services – ultimately serving their customers' specific needs.

The best way to start building product knowledge is by believing in the merit of one's own products.

This means the salesperson should not only use the product for themselves (if feasible), but also have a real belief in what it is that they are selling, as well as in in the company's overall vision and mission. To take this dedication a step further, test out a competitor's product for a firsthand comparison with the one your company is selling.

It should also be noted that a dedicated salesperson does not solely rely on company training in order to gain product knowledge. They keep themselves updated for any newly added features so that they are able to build on their arsenal of information. Doing so will allow you to develop a competitive edge against sales representatives from rival companies and in turn, increase your sales quota.

Your business card and a brochure won't do the selling for you.

Customers need an intuitive understanding regarding your products and services. It is wise to remember that the written word and the spoken word do not always convey the same meaning, and even when they do, the spoken word can allow for added passion and conviction when delivered correctly. So, do not just hand over the sales literature and expect a callback from a potential customer. Instead, take time to explain in detail what your products and services have to offer that your competitors offerings do not. It's also wise to encourage frank customer feedback during a sales pitch, so that you can find out about any shortcomings of whatever it is you are selling. Having an understanding of how your customer sees your product allows you to understand if there are improvements to be made, either in the product or service itself, or in the way you are attempting to sell it.

Always cater to each customer specifically.

It's vitally important for your sales pitches to not only cover the advantages and benefits of your product or service, but also to explain how can they meet the requirements of the customer's specific requirements. That is where comprehensive product knowledge comes handy because this will enable a salesperson to tailor their words according to the needs of the specific customer they are selling to.

You are not selling a product or a service; you are selling a solution.

Your customers are not looking to buy something they don't need, nor do they want to buy an innovation or some "groundbreaking feature". What's more, they have no interest whatsoever in the commission you'll be making if the sale goes through!

The important thing to keep in mind when attempting to sell is the psychological nuances that will hook customers, and how to make them feel that they are paying for something that will make their life easier or better. A customer might be buying a better experience, more time saved when doing something, increased chances of achieving a desired outcome, a certain lifestyle or more quality time with loved ones. In other words, the thing that the customer will buy is simply a vehicle to attain a desired outcome. The importance of understanding this point cannot be overstated! As a salesperson, it is your job to know exactly what your customers want, then show them how your product or service will assist in getting them there. As the saying goes, "No one wants a drill; they want a hole." Let that be the approach for all your sales pitches.

As a final point for this chapter, think about this; when was the last time a salesperson simply said to a customer, "Buy this!", and the customer happily complied? The answer to this question (and I hope you already know this!) is never. That's because selling is an art form to be mastered, and one crucial component is a thorough understanding of your product or service, as well as the ability to convey these benefits in a way which convinces the customer that they should part with their money in order to obtain the advantage that your product or service offers

In the next chapter we'll take a closer look at obtaining customer confidence and why it's important to make the customer feel like their interests come first.

Chapter 2

The Customer Comes First

How to get customers to trust you

Trust is an important ingredient whenever a salesperson is attempting to win a customer over. So how does one go about establishing this trust? Knowing what you are selling inside and out is only one part of the equation. You need to also learn to think like your customers.

It's about them, not you.

Whenever you try to pitch a product or service, the customer or client will undoubtedly be thinking, "What's in it for me?". Paradoxical as it may seem, selling has to involve a genuine concern and desire to help customers with their specific problems first and foremost; the commission that you are going to make if the sale goes through should be put to the back of your mind. Cultivate a genuine mentality of "the customer comes first", and you will find yourself naturally building a connection and establishing rapport with your customers.

Don't fake it.

Fake concerns are always apparent and people will usually eventually be able to sense them, if not consciously then subconsciously. It's important as a salesperson not to adopt a "slippery" or "slimy" personality; the customer *will* be put off by it. Instead focus on the facts and let the customers know how your products or services will cater to their needs.

Do your research and be prepared.

As discussed in the previous chapter, knowing your product is important, but this alone is not enough;

you also need to familiarize yourself with who you are selling to. That means knowing their target market, as well as having some information on the individual customers you will be pitching sales to if possible. Only then can you most effectively know how your products and services can provide useful solutions to these specific customers. This will also make it easier for you to tailor your sales pitch in an attempt to sell these solutions to the customer.

Never be afraid to ask questions.

Sometimes as a salesperson, one feels embarrassed to ask questions for fear of coming off as incompetent in the customers eyes. This however is oftentimes a mistake. Never be afraid to ask questions especially when you need customers to clarify something. Asking questions also shows that you are attentive and would like to learn more about the customers specific needs.

Use questions to gather information which you can then use to position your products or services more effectively. Asking effective questions is definitely an art. Oftentimes, salesmen and women are impatient and wrongfully assume that they understand the nature of their customers' problems. It is important to ask the correct questions to get a better understanding of the needs of one's customers, and also to make an effort to fully understand their problems before attempting to solve them.

Ask questions that will make your prospects aware of the consequences of their action or inaction.

It is always important to remember as a salesperson, you will never be able to convince a customer by force or by overtly goading them. It's okay to be assertive, but always remember not to push the customers so hard that they decide to completely back away from buying. It is important to come across as non-threatening, and informative, making the customers aware of the benefits and consequences of their particular actions or inactions when it comes to the opportunity you're offering them.

Focus on the long-term.

Some salespeople become repetitive, and at times even desperate, during a pitch as they get too fixated on making the sale. A salesperson should always bear in mind that it is not just about completing a sale, but in addition to this it is the rapport that one is able to build that will keep a customer coming back. It helps for a salesperson to remind themselves to also keep the bigger picture in mind, rather than simply focusing on the sole objective of meeting their sales quota in the short term. If you become fixated on the short term payout you may ruin the opportunity to create a long-lasting relationship which could pay dividends down the road. Know when to delay gratification for the bigger long term payout!

Be direct.

There are times when it's necessary to be elaborate, but more often than not, simplicity is the key to success. Preparing elaborate and complicated sales presentation can confuse customers with too much information. It's sometimes more effective to simply be direct and concise with the information that one shares with customers. Being too fancy and beating around the bush can work against you, not to mention, you run the risk of coming off as untrustworthy. Sometimes it is better to keep things simple and stick to the facts.

Sell your team.

Customers are not only prompted to buy something solely due to a product's merit; the feelings of trust that they get from the salesperson who is attempting to sell that product or service can also play a part in their decision to buy. It's always worth bearing in mind that even though humans are rational creatures, we are also emotionally driven, and oftentimes emotions hold more weight than rationality. A salesperson who is able to gain the trust and respect of a customer will always out perform those who just focus solely on selling, and ignore the importance of creating meaningful connections with their customers.

Follow up with the customer, but don't overdo it.

While it is a good idea to follow up with a potential customer, take care that your persistence does not cross the line and become an annoyance. There are times when following up is important, but a salesperson should strive for a balance of being persistent without coming across as annoying.

Make your prospects feel like you care for their well-being rather than giving them the impression that you are simply after their hard-earned money. As well as being emotional creatures, we are also social creatures. Most of the time, people, whether they are aware of it at the time or not, want to feel like they are being cared for; for others to show them concern and make them feel understood. As a salesperson, one should aim to focus on showing genuine concern and readiness to help customers with their problems.

Hopefully this chapter has helped clarify exactly why it is important to put the customer first. In the following chapter we'll go on to look more closely at the importance of knowing your market.

Chapter 3

Know Your Market

Understanding your customers'

needs better

It is always important to evaluate the needs of your target market. Trends change, competitors come and go, as will the demands of you potential customers. Bearing in mind that what works today may not be relevant tomorrow, an up to date knowledge of what your target market needs will go a long way in tailoring your products and services to accommodate market demand.

Evaluate your market constantly and act fast.

In actuality, there is an abundance of options available to your potential customers from your competitors. Hence, don't get cocky, even if the economy is booming and business is regular. It is a human's natural tendency to be complacent when good things are happening, but the truth is that when things are good, it is critical to be more cautious. In the competitive business arena, your survival can only be ensured by keeping an eye on your target market and adapt accordingly. That means upgrading and improving your products and services, and also reevaluating you sales strategy accordingly.

Salespeople can also take on the role of market researchers. Since they deal directly with customers, they may just be the best people to identify and troubleshoot their problems. Dedicated salespeople are also aware of ongoing trends, and are therefore often able to contribute as far as envisioning what could happen in the company's future, and in turn, how they could upgrade their products.

This process can be initiated by shifting one's focus from merely delivering information and selling to prospective customers, to taking a keen interest in customer needs by asking smart questions that gauge what they are looking for and how your products and services can be improved upon to better fit their needs.

Good salespeople add value via the selling process.

There is no point in hiring salespeople to only pass on information to potential customers. While information is always useful, any buyer is capable of doing this research for themselves. In addition, they are likely to have already compared what you are selling with the options your competitors are offering. The best salespeople are not only bearers of information, they are also expert problem-solvers. They know how to connect what their customers need with what they are selling, and are able to further educate their customers beyond just the basics of their products.

Remember that buyers are not just looking for people to supply them with basic information and sell them something; they are looking for solutions to their problems. Since most consumers are bombarded with massive amounts of information, they are most likely to opt for a doing business with a company they trust. It is up to the salesperson to use their expertise to meet the needs of their customers, and find opportunities to solve the problems via the use of their products and services. Simply put, as a salesperson, your job is to put a human face to a business, and forge a connection with your market.

A salesperson becomes indispensable when they are able to provide genuine assistance that a customer is satisfied with. Become a force for progress, not only within the company, but also with your customers.

Remember that you are dealing with a smart and informed market.

It is safe to assume that consumers nowadays are smart, educated people. They are oftentimes independent and self-sufficient, and prefer to do their own research in order to help them decide what they should spending their hard-earned money on. This allows for them to save themselves not only money, but also time and effort in the long run. The fact is, they may not really need a salesperson to pitch for them; what they really need is someone knowledgeable enough to be able to answer some lingering questions and offer sound advice.

It is then, safe to assume that buyers will be more than happy to listen to a salesperson they deem trustworthy, comes across as intelligent and knowledgable, and knows what they are selling. As a salesperson, one must be empathetic, able to put customers first, and able to understand the big picture.

Never underestimate integrity.

Professional credibility is important, but it is extra important to build deep personal trust with one's customers. Integrity is always a great asset when working in sales as it proves that not only are you are able to prioritize your clients, you are able to perform reliably and consistently. Seller-buyer relationships built on integrity and trust are important because they lessen the risk of unnecessary conflict and misunderstandings, along with missed deadlines and other trivial problems that may occur.

Diversify the way you reach out to your target market.

The preferences of consumers vary greatly nowadays. Some may prefer to buy over the internet as this can be more convenient, while others prefer the conventional method of buying face to face. There are also those who prefer a mixture of the two.

In the digital era that we live in, it may be tempting to bring all your selling activities online, eliminating the need for face to face salespeople and print advertising. You may be under the impression that the traditional brochure has become outdated, but in reality it plays an important role in a marketing strategy. A brochure has better readability compared to any web sites, which will require the use of a mobile device or a laptop.

Well-written sales literature, coupled with a winning pitch has the power to create a strong lasting impression. So, it's always a great idea to take advantage of the conventional method of reaching out to customers, as well as supplementing this approach with multimedia marketing materials. However good the new methods may be, there really is no substitute for the human factor.

Always aim to get free word-of-mouth advertising from satisfied customers.

Usually, when customers are pleased with a salesperson, they are more than likely to refer the salesperson to others. However, it is crucial for the salesperson to approach the subject of referrals, (assuming they believe their customer was happy with the service or product the received).

It is better for the salesperson to refrain from asking questions which are overly direct, such as whether their customer would know anyone who would also like to buy what they are selling, as such an approach may come off as intrusive and pushy.

In order to successfully obtain referrals, it is critical for the salesperson to be specific in their approach and offer solutions to customers instead of a catalogue of goods and services. Additionally, offering a small reward for customer who provide you with referrals – such as discounts or small gifts – can also be helpful in expanding your clientele.

Chapter 4

Overcoming The Fear Of Rejection

It's bound to happen and you need to deal it!

As a salesperson, rejection is an inevitable part of the job. Sometimes, no matter how good your pitch is, you can't do anything when the customer simply refuses to make a purchase. However, you should never allow yourself to become discouraged. Instead, strive to do better next time, and never let the fear of getting rejected stand in your way of continuing to attempt to make sales.

Know your sales ratio.

As a salesperson, it's important to know one's own sales ratio, since the number will be different depending on what one is selling. While it isn't difficult to figure out the numbers within one's business, talking to other people and gathering information, as well as being observant about one's success rate will enable a salesperson to estimate just how many rejections they should expect. Going in with a realistic estimate of the sales ratio you can expect to achieve can help prevent rejections from bringing your spirits down.

Set long-term goals.

Having personal goals will also enable you to develop a strong mindset and cope better with sales rejections. Goals enable a salesperson to think beyond the short-term objectives, such as monthly quotas and annual targets, and shift focus to ultimately more important areas such as the company's larger vision. It will enable you to stay focused and retain your determination in the face of rejections.

Don't take it personally.

At the end of the day, we are human. We strive to be accepted and validated. Sometimes when we experience rejection, we can't help but to take it personally. Oftentimes we feel that a rejection robs us of our self-worth. We blame ourselves continuously for our failures. However, failures only show us exactly where we needs to improve. Whenever a salesperson experiences a rejection, they should aim to learn from the experience and use it as a form of self improvement.

Failure to make a sale may not be entirely your fault. There are times when you may encounter customers whom, regardless of how good your sales pitch is, will not buy what you are selling. It does not mean that you are incompetent, or that they are simply wasting your time. Maybe they do not have a strong enough need for what you are selling at the moment, or they simply cannot afford to buy it. In such cases, you should strive to build rapport with the customer. For all you know, they may just come back to you in future when the need arises or when they have the means. You may even obtain referrals from a non-buying potential customer.

Get into a routine.

Developing a routine can steady a salesperson's mind and allow him or her to stay motivated. Routines can help center our minds so that we can find it easier to stay in a state of harmony and flow. Since things happen to throw us off from time to time, having a routine will help keep us calm and focused. Furthermore, following a routine enables us to get into the habit of regularly repeating our actions and, assuming we stick to our plan, master certain tasks. When you have a routine set out for your sales work, you'll more than likely feel better prepared to cope with difficulties and a rejection may feel like no more than a speed bump, rather than a major disaster.

Build relationships.

It is important not to be embittered when a prospective buyer rejects your offer. In the business world, interpersonal relationships are equally, if not more, important than making a sale. Who knows when a once prospective buyer will show up again to actually make a purchase from you? Build rapport, and as they say, "Keep the conversation going."

A salesperson can also establish themselves by doing extra little things that the majority are not doing. Examples are writing articles, or even creating newsletters. This will not only help you connect with the target market but can also add to your credibility. Establishing oneself will allow a salesperson to foster trust among customers.

Take time to acknowledge your accomplishments.

Acknowledging your accomplishments will not only give you a boost, it will also enable you to have a better understanding of the progress that you are making. You will be come to know where your strengths are, as well as determining where you need to improve and what you need to work on.

While it is not wise to get drunk on success, it is prudent to acknowledge it and keep striving to improve. After all, having confidence in oneself is the first and most vital ingredient on the path to becoming a success. Positivity and the right mindset may be overstated at times, but they certainly affect the overall psyche of a salesperson and this positive mindset can be detected by potential customers.

Learn to be your own motivational coach.

Use positive self-talk to help you get through a rough patch. A simple way to do this is to keep reminding yourself that one rejection does not mean you have failed. Remind yourself to stay focused on the bigger picture, and accept that rejections and short term setbacks are just one of the hurdles to selling. Then, pick yourself back up and move on to the next challenge.

Come to terms with the fact that you can't please everyone all the time, no matter how good of a salesperson you are.

While it is a good practice to evaluate your products, services and sales strategies on a regular basis, dwelling too much on rejections can be detrimental to your overall success. It is a reality that in business, as in life, no matter how hard we try, we cannot please everyone. There are bound to be customers who will never have a need for what you are selling, however great your products or services may be.

It's easy to shrug off the first few rejections, but when they begin to pile up and the numbers start increasing, a sense of panic can start to set in. If you are looking to minimize your rejection rate, it would pay to evaluate your target customers and the overall market you are selling to. In other words, you need to better redefine your target market. There is no point in targeting customers who do not need or can't afford to buy from you. Tighten your focus and concentrate your energy on those who are most likely to be interested in what you are selling. The "80-20" principle is real, and more often than not a business will make the vast majority of its profits (about 80% according to the 80-20 principle) from a core group of customers, (the 20% in the 80-20).

Avoid getting emotionally invested in a particular customer.

When a salesperson cares about a prospect who rejected them, he or she might take it more personally. The level of involvement can determine the level of despair when rejection occurs. The best way to avoid letting one potential customer who slipped away get you down is to rethink your approach, and treat all customers as equals. Do not single out a few customers as special in your mind because they led you to believe your dealings with them would more than likely lead to a sale. Remember, a sale is never confirmed until money changes hands.

Every sales person has experienced rejection.

It is important not to take rejection personally. It is an inevitability in the lives of everyone who has ever tried to sell something. There may be times when things happen, expectedly or unexpectedly, that causes a customer to turn down your offer. Like every job, there are going to be bad days. Perhaps the economy is not doing so well or the customers company experienced unforeseen difficulties. It's up to the salesperson to decide how to internalize such events, and whether to give up or to give oneself the permission to fail and just weather this temporary set back. In the end, we can't always control what goes around us, but we do have full control over our own reactions and attitude toward it.

Chapter 5

The Effortless Close

Overcome objections and seal the

deal

In order to successfully close a sale, there are some tried-and-tested techniques that have proven to be vital for success. There is however no magic formula to guarantee that a salesperson will be able to make a sale, and as established in the previous chapter, rejections will happen from time to time. However, the tips and tricks highlighted here are key concepts to selling and,when properly implemented, will heighten your chances of successfully clinching a deal.

Opinions count.

Asking the customer for their opinion can prove to be a vital component in closing a sale. Asking this question enables the customer to air his or her thoughts in regard to the product, without having to worry about objections.

When a customer discloses their opinions, a good salesperson will be able to use this information to analyze the customer's needs more deeply. This in turn will allow the salesperson to assist the customer more fully thus increasing the chances of both making a sale as well as creating a stronger bond with the customer.

Sharp angle close.

Whenever a customer inquires about a concession, such as free delivery, a price reduction, or some other request, take this as an opportunity in order to close a sale, by stating, "If I am able to do that for you today, will you be able to commit to making a purchase?"

This is a great closing question! Not only will it give the customer an incentive to take action and agree to a sale, it will also give them the feeling that you have reached a win-win outcome, thus increasing the quality of the bond between you which may lead to further business opportunities in the future.

Assumptive close.

If a salesperson has formed a relationship with a customer, the customer will oftentimes respect his or her judgment. A salesperson should be able to provide the customer with products and services that serve their needs. After doing so, in order to close the sale, the salesperson should offer to choose option which is best suited to the customer's particular requirements, from a list of options previously discussed. Again, this will usually only work if a salesperson has formed a relationship with a customer, but when this relationship has been formed it can lead to a massive reduction in a customers resistance to make a purchase. This is another example of why it's always important to aim to build relationships with your customers whenever possible.

Something for nothing.

A good technique, though rather gimmicky, is for a salesperson to throw in something that was not part of the original agreement in order to "sweeten the deal".

For example, when closing a sale, consider offering to throw in an additional item free of charge if the customer will make a purchase immediately or within a set period of time. Although the item itself may not have a great monetary value, everyone loves something for nothing and offering a complimentary product or service free of charge can make the difference between making a sale or missing out.

"The Ben Franklin".

From the great Benjamin Franklin himself, this technique involves, "listing two columns, the pros and cons, and basing one's choice on the longer column." This approach is particularly useful when dealing with customers who have more analytical personalities. It can be cleverly employed as a closing technique by filling up the "pro" column and clearly spelling out the benefits your product or service offers. Just make sure that the customer won't be able to come up with too many "cons"!

The porcupine.

This technique also allows you to gauge a customers interest as well as enabling you to gather more information about their needs. When a customer asks for an item and says, for example, "Does this come in the color green?" rather than answering directly, consider replying with, "Would you like it in green?".

This answer allows the customer to provide more thoughtful answers regarding their needs, which will in turn enable the salesperson to adjust his or her presentation accordingly. This technique can be especially useful when you have the feeling that a customer is not clear on exactly what it is they are looking for. Use this line of questioning carefully and don't overdo it.

Solicit objections.

After going through the discovery phase of the sales cycle, and you're certain that the customer has a level of understanding of the product or service you are offering, and assuming they seem interested, you may be able to move to soliciting objections. An example of the kind of question you could ask in order to solicit objections could be, "Is there any reason why we cannot proceed with the shipment?" Taking this route flips the sales process on it's head, as rather than trying to convince the customer to buy you are asking them (in an indirect manner) for reasons they would not buy thus taking the onus off of yourself and putting it onto the customer. Timing is important here as you need to be reasonably sure that the customer is interested in making a purchase before attempting this technique.

Direct Close.

When you have addressed your customer's concerns and have absolute certainty that the customer knows the value of the products or services on offer, it's often best to simply ask directly, "So, are you ready to place an order?" This directness shows confidence on the part of the salesperson and can creates a level of trust and a sense of urgency in the customer that can convince them to go ahead with placing an order order. Of course, this is a close-ended question, so it's important to feel at least reasonably confident that the answer you'll hear back from the customer will be a positive one!

Closing a sale is an art form in itself and a good salesperson needs to have a good feel for both when and how to close. Be aware of the feedback you're getting from the customer and decide on an appropriate method of closing in accordance to this feedback. Also, timing is everything; try to close the sale too soon and you risk scaring the customer off, too late and you may miss your window of opportunity!

In the next chapter you'll have an opportunity to assess your strengths and weaknesses as a salesperson.

Chapter 6

Assess your strengths and weaknesses

How good are your current sales skills?

It's important for any salesperson to have an honest understanding of what they are doing right and what they could work on in order to become a more effective salesperson. In this chapter, I'll be asking twenty questions which I suggest you give some though to as I invite you to take an honest look at your own strengths and weaknesses. Only by understanding where we are coming up short can we hope to improve and evolve.

As mentioned, I recommend you spend some time really thinking deeply about each of the questions in this chapter. Not only that, but get out a pen and some notepaper and jot down your thoughts. When you have an idea of the areas you need to work on, go back and jot down some actionable steps you can take to improve and then go about implementing those ideas as soon as possible. Check back in on a regular basis and reassess yourself honestly to gauge whether or not you're improving.

1. Do I possess the required knowledge to be the best salesperson I can be? Am I well-informed, not only about my own company and product but also

about the prospective customer's company and specific pain points?

2. Am I an effective communicator? Am I capable of articulating your thoughts in an easily comprehensible manner? Am I being clear and concise in what I'm communicating?

3. How disciplined am I? Do I have the unrelenting attitude in my sales approach that will allow me to go above and beyond and do whatever it takes to close a deal? How can I cultivate a more disciplined work ethic?

4. Am I as charismatic as I could be? Do I have the required charisma to form a sense of connection and understanding between myself and my prospects? How could I become more charismatic?

5. Do I have the required confidence in myself, my company and the products I sell to be the most effective sales person I can be? Do I act fearlessly and am I willing to take risks without worrying about hearing a "no" from a customer or losing out on a potential opportunity? How can I improve in this regard?

6. Am I firm enough when it comes to sales? Do I demonstrate this firmness when making follow-up

calls with both potential customers and prospects who have said no?

7. Am I resourceful? Do I go above and beyond the obvious and use every resource or asset at my disposal to close a deal? What assets or resources am I not taking full advantage of?

8. Am I able to think critically? Rather than following a set script when aiming to make a sale, am I able to adapt and alter my sales pitches in accordance with the prospective customer, time and place?

9. Am I coming across as overly desperate when attempting to make a sale? Am I giving the customer the impression that they would be doing me a service by buying my product or am I giving the customer the feeling the one that they are the one with the most to gain from the transaction?

10. How do I react to hearing the word, "no"? Do I immediately feel anxious or defeated, or does the know give me a feeling of excitement and give me a buzz in anticipation of the challenge of convincing the customer to change their mind?

11. Do I show the required persistence and dogged determination when receiving negative responses? Am I able to approach prospects from different

angles when necessary? When do I need to show more determination?

12. Do I have full trust in my team? Are their any issues or concerns I need to raise with my teammates in order to build a better, stronger and more productive relationship with them?

13. Am I being as open-minded as I could be? In addition to this, am I demonstrating a willingness to listen, or am I simply berating prospects with an overwhelming flood of information? Where should I be doing less talking and more listening, showing an open-mind to whatever problems the prospective customer is trying to overcome?

14. Am I writing down my sales goals clearly and regularly? When I have challenges which I don't immediately understand the cause of, am I taking the time to direct them and get to the root cause so as to be able to avoid them cropping up again in the future?

15. Am I being honest about the about the product or service I'm trying to sell? Do I ever feed potential customers lies or undeliverable promises? How could I improve in this respect?

16. Do I have a genuine passion for and belief in the product I am selling? If not, how can I become more passionate about it?

17. Am I being curious? Am I constantly looking to learn more about my product, my potential customers and how I can bridge the gap between both parties?

18. How focused am I in my work life? Am I able to concentrate on a given task without becoming overwhelmed or distracted? How might a lack of focus be impacting my sales performance?

19. Are my closing skills as good as they could be? Do I ever do most of the hard work in a sales pitch only for my close to let me down? How could I be a better closer?

20. Am I showing a healthy competitive drive? Am I constantly striving to be the top salesperson within my company (and within the industry!)? Am I setting the proverbial bar as high as possible, and giving myself lofty targets to shoot for, understanding that even if I miss these ambitious targets, I will still be well-positioned to achieve great things?

Make sure you give each of these questions some real thought. Refer back to instances in the past and think about how you could have done things better. Even if you feel things are going well, there is almost always room for improvement. How could you be a better salesperson? What steps could you implement to start moving from good to great? Make sure you write down your ideas and refer back to them regularly to check in on your progress.

I hope this chapter has helped shed light on where your strengths and weaknesses lie in terms of your sales ability. In the final chapter I've included some thought-provoking words of wisdom from some truly remarkable individuals

Chapter 7

Words of wisdom

Inspirational and motivational quotes

related to sales

In this final chapter, I'd like to leave you with some food for thought. The following quotes are from some of the most successful salespeople and businessmen who have ever lived. By listening to what these people have to say on the topic we are effectively standing on the shoulders of giants; learning from those who have already excelled in this area.

While many of the quotes may at first glance seen to hold a nothing more than a simple message, I suggest you think deeply about each one and ask yourself if there may be something you can take from these words of wisdom. Be honest with yourself and for each of the quotes, think about where you are, and perhaps where you're not, implementing the ideas which are being presented. Reflect on these ideas regularly and try to keep them in mind during your working day.

Make a customer, not a sale.

Katherine Barchetti

Tough times never last, but tough people do.

Robert Schuller

Most of the important things in the world have been accomplished by people who have kept on trying when there seemed to be no hope at all.

Dale Carnegie

Lack of direction, not lack of time, is the problem. We all have twenty-four hour days.

Zig Ziglar

Integrity is what we do, what we say and what we say we do.

Don Galer

Don't wish it were easier, wish you were better.

Jim Rohn

He that is good for making excuses is seldom good for anything else.

Benjamin Franklin

Fear is the destroyer of dreams and the killer of ambitions.

Jeffrey Benjamin

The questions you ask are more important than the things you could ever say.

Tom Freese

Excellence is not a skill. It's an attitude.

Ralph Marston

Today is always the most productive

day of your week.

Mark Hunter

Goals allow you to control the direction

of change in your favour.

Brian Tracy

For every sale you miss because you're too enthusiastic, you will miss a hundred because you're not enthusiastic enough.

Zig Ziglar

Try not to become a person of success, but try to become a person of value.

Albert Einstein

Self-pity is an acid which eats holes in happiness.

Earl Nightingale

Your competition is EVERYTHING else your prospect could conceivably spend their money on.

Don Cooper

If people like you, they'll listen to you, but if they trust you, they'll do business with you.

Zig Ziglar

Prospecting - Find the man with the problem.

Ben Friedman

If opportunity doesn't knock, build a door.

Milton Berle

The way you position yourself at the beginning of a relationship has profound impact on where you end up.

Ron Karr

Every brand isn't for everybody, and everybody isn't for every brand.

Liz Lange

The most unprofitable item ever manufactured is an excuse.

John Mason

Success is the culmination of failures, mistakes, false starts, confusion, and the determination to keep going anyway.

Nick Gleason

Most people think "selling" is the same as "talking". But the most effective salespeople know that listening is the most important part of their job.

Roy Bartell

You don't close a sale; you open a relationship if you want to build a long-term, successful enterprise.

Patricia Fripp

If you are not taking care of your customer, your competitor will.

Bob Hooey

There are no shortcuts to any place worth going.

Beverly Sills

Life's battles don't always go to the strongest or fastest; sooner or later those who win are those who think they can.

Richard Bach

If we learn from losing, we become winners in the end.

Anonymous

If we all did the things we are capable of doing, we would literally astound ourselves.

Thomas Edison

Obstacles can't stop you. Problems can't stop you. Most of all, other people can't stop you. Only you can stop you.

Jeffrey Gitomer

Leadership is doing what is right when no one is watching.

George Van Valkenburg

Great works are performed not by strength but by perseverance.

Samuel Johnson

Success is the ability to go from failure to failure without losing your enthusiasm.

Winston Churchill

Some men see things as they are and ask why...I dream of things that never were and ask why not?

Robert Kennedy

Failure will never overtake me if my determination to succeed is strong enough.

Og Mandino

Opportunities are usually disguised as hard work, so most people don't recognize them.

Ann Landers

The majority of men meet with failure because of their lack of persistence in creating new plans to take the place of those which fail.

Napoleon Hill

You can do anything if you have enthusiasm. Enthusiasm is the yeast that makes your hopes rise to the stars. With it, there is accomplishment. Without it there are only alibis.

Henry Ford

Do not let what you cannot do interfere with what you can do.

John Wooden

Take risks. If you win, you'll be happy;

if you lose, you'll be wise.

Anonymous

Don't be distracted by criticism.

Remember the only taste of success

some people have is when they take a

bite out of you.

Zig Ziglar

The best sales questions have your expertise wrapped into them.

Jill Konrath

Make a customer, not a sale.

Katherine Barchetti

Tough times never last, but tough people do.

Robert Schuller

Most of the important things in the world have been accomplished by people who have kept on trying when there seemed to be no hope at all.

Dale Carnegie

Lack of direction, not lack of time, is the problem. We all have twenty-four hour days.

Zig Ziglar

Integrity is what we do, what we say and what we say we do.

Don Galer

Don't wish it were easier, wish you were better.

Jim Rohn

He that is good for making excuses is seldom good for anything else.

Benjamin Franklin

Fear is the destroyer of dreams and the killer of ambitions.

Jeffrey Benjamin

The questions you ask are more important than the things you could ever say.

Tom Freese

Excellence is not a skill. It's an attitude.

Ralph Marston

Today is always the most productive day of your week.

Mark Hunter

Goals allow you to control the direction of change in your favour.

Brian Tracy

For every sale you miss because you're too enthusiastic, you will miss a hundred because you're not enthusiastic enough.

Zig Ziglar

**Try not to become a person of success,
but try to become a person of value.**

Albert Einstein

**Self-pity is an acid which eats holes in
happiness.**

Earl Nightingale

**Your competition is EVERYTHING else
your prospect could conceivably spend
their money on.**

Don Cooper

If people like you, they'll listen to you, but if they trust you, they'll do business with you.

Zig Ziglar

Prospecting - Find the man with the problem.

Ben Friedman

If opportunity doesn't knock, build a door.

Milton Berle

The way you position yourself at the beginning of a relationship has profound impact on where you end up.

Ron Karr

It's easier to explain price once than to apologize for quality forever.

Zig Ziglar

A good listener is not only popular everywhere, but after a while he knows something.

Wilson Mizner

Goals aren't enough. You need goals plus deadlines: goals big enough to get excited about and deadline to make you run. One isn't much good without the other, but together they can be tremendous.

Ben Feldman

You will never find time for anything. If you want time you must make it.

Charles Robert Buxton

The difference between a successful person and others is not a lack of strength, not a lack of knowledge, but rather a lack of will.

Vince Lombardi

The man who will use his skill and constructive imagination to see how much he can give for a dollar, instead of how little he can give for a dollar, is bound to succeed.

Henry Ford

The difference between try and triumph

is just a little umph!

Marvin Phillips

<u>Conclusion</u>

In this book, I hope I have managed to give you some new perspectives on sales and specifically how to become a better salesperson. As described over the previous chapters, sales is truly an art form where reading the customer and adjusting your approach are of vital importance. In addition, I hope you now also have an appreciation of the importance of both timing and building relationships.

Prepare as well as you can, remember to stay focused, confident and positive, and with practice you will be able to master the art of selling. Good luck!

A message from the author, Steve Gold

Thank you for your purchase of this book. If you enjoyed it, **please** take the time to share your thoughts and post a review on Amazon. It will only take a couple of minutes and I'd be extremely grateful for your support.

Thank you again.

Steve Gold

FREE BONUS!: Preview Of "Elon Musk - The Biography of a Modern Day Renaissance Man"!

The Biography Of A Modern Day Renaissance Man

If you enjoyed this book, I have a little bonus for you; a preview of one of my other books "Elon Musk - The Biography of a Modern Day Renaissance Man". In this book, I take a closer look at exactly who Elon Musk is as well as examining the truly extraordinary accomplishments he has managed to achieve. Enjoy the free sample, and feel free to click on the purchase link below if you would like to learn more about this truly incredible individual!

Introduction

When actor Robert Downey Jr. signed on to portray Tony Stark (a.k.a. Iron Man), he suggested to director John Favreau that they meet up with Elon Musk. They have a task of bringing to life a superhero, and Musk is the closest there ever is to Marvel's genius, billionaire, philanthropist in real life. The meeting was set and some of Musk's characteristics went into RDJ's portrayal of Tony Stark on screen, thus creating the memorable character that people come to know and love.

In reality, there is far more to Musk's life and person than can be personified by a fictional character. Sure, he does have a lot in common with Iron Man; he's a prodigious tech genius and entrepreneur, with the capacity to make seemingly impossible ideas a reality. Like Tony Stark, he dreams, thinks and lives large, but that is where the similarity ends.

Unlike his comic book counterpart, Elon Musk was not born into a life of luxury and ease. Despite showing potential for greatness as early as his preteens, his childhood and young adult life was filled with adversaries. To this day, Musk credits his early life struggles in helping him cultivate the indomitable spirit he is known for.

Having made his mark in the field of IT, finance, sustainable energy, automotive, aerospace manufacturing and space exploration, it is an understatement to say that Musk has come a long way from his humble beginnings. He founded some of the most pioneering companies – Paypal, Tesla Motors, and SpaceX – and is almost single-handed responsible for each enterprise's success. Whichever business he decided to dabble in, he brought with him a revolutionary idea which often ends up being a game-changer in the industry. Yet, he is far from done.

His brilliant mind never ceased to think up grander innovations, even after numerous repeated successful endeavors. His ample and wild ambitions, it seems, are driven by grand visions of changing the world we live in. His agenda for the future includes filling the roads with more electric cars, powering the world with solar energy, colonizing neighboring planets and enabling people to cover great distances with a futuristic high-speed public transportation system.

Most children would imagine of going outer space and travel to different cities in bullet-fast capsule pods, until those fantasies fade away in adulthood. Rarely are there individuals who dare to dream of living those fantasies that appropriately should stay within the realm of fiction. Elon Musk is among the exceptional few.

Chapter 1

The Beginnings Of Greatness

Almost every success story of high-achieving individuals contain episodes highlighting their extraordinary iron will, critical thinking, propensity for hard work, and an unwavering belief that the impossible is not out of their reach. As one of the most brilliant minds who help shaped the global economy after at the dawn of the information age and tech boom in the late 20th century, it is hardly surprising that Elon Musk displayed such distinctive personality traits at an incredibly young age.

Elon Reeve Musk was born in June 28 of 1971, in Pretoria, Gauteng, South Africa. His father is a South African-born British electrical engineer, Errol Musk, and his mother is Canadian-English dietitian, Maye Musk. Elon is the eldest of their three children, followed by brother Kimbal and sister Tosca.

Growing up in Pretoria, Elon's early years were far from a picture perfect childhood. His parents divorced when he was 9 years-old, after which he lived mostly with his demanding and emotionally abusive father. At school, he endured harsh bullying by his peers. In one notable instance, he ended up hospitalized after being pushed down a flight of stairs. Such ordeals led Elon to find solace in the safest company available; his own thoughts and imagination which resided in the deep recesses of his prodigious mind.

He would regularly immerse himself in reading as a means of escaping his troubles in the outside world. Encyclopedias and science fiction were among his favorite books; they added to his knowledge bank and encouraged his seemingly wild dreams of futuristic technology which had yet to become a reality. Often times, Elon would be caught daydreaming and lost in his own thoughts, ignoring the world around him in favor of the utopias in his imagination. Along with his innovative thoughts, Elon's childhood experiences also contributed to him developing a high tolerance for hardship and an extraordinary work ethic; attributes which he is well known for and which have served him well in his life.

His aptitude for technological innovations and entrepreneurship was evident when he began teaching himself computer programming at the tender age of 10. When he was just 12, he developed a spaceship shooter video game called, "Blastar", which he sold to a computer magazine for $500. After his first brush with success, Elon and his younger brother, Kimbal, hatched a plan to open an arcade near their school. Unfortunately, their enterprising plan had to be scrapped when their parents refused to provide the legal consent to obtain a business permit.

In 1988, after graduating from Pretoria Boys High School at the age of 17, Elon made the momentous decision to leave his hometown for the United States, without the support of his parents. This would be the first step towards his hard-earned success. He was able to obtain Canadian citizenship through his mother a year later, and left South Africa for

Montreal, Canada. There, he worked low-paying jobs and was living on the brink of poverty for a year.

At the age of 19, he was accepted into Queens University in Kingston, Ontario for undergraduate studies in science. It was during his studies that he met Canadian author, Justine Musk, whom he would marry in 2000 and end up having six sons with. Their marriage lasted for only eight years, and Elon got married for the second time to British actress Talulah Riley. This marriage ended in divorce in 2014.

Two years into his studies at Queens, Elon received a scholarship from The University of Pennsylvania (Penn) in America. He relocated to the US in 1992, following his transfer to Penn. In the following year, he earned his Bachelor of Science degree in Physics from Penn's College of Arts and Sciences, and stayed back a year at Penn's Wharton School to complete his studies for a Bachelor of Science degree in Economics.

Throughout his college years, alongside his scientific studies, Elon took a keen interest in philosophical and religious literature. It was stated that his all-time favorite book is *The Hitchhiker's Guide to the Galaxy* by Douglas Adams. It is through this immersion in both science and personal studies of humanities that Elon found his calling; he had the lofty ambition of wanting to contribute to projects that would change the world for the better.

Consequently, his vision and entrepreneurial aspirations began taking shape, specifically in the areas of the internet, renewable energy and space exploration.

Check out the rest of "Elon Musk - The Biography of a Modern Day Renaissance Man" on Amazon.

Check Out My Other Books!

Elon Musk - The Biography Of A Modern Day Renaissance Man

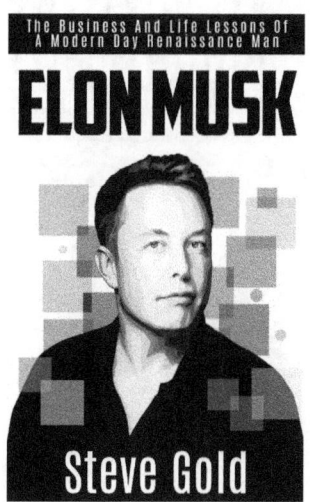

Elon Musk - The Business & Life Lessons Of A Modern Day Renaissance Man

**Warren Buffett - The Business And Life
Lessons Of An Investment Genius, Magnate
And Philanthropist**

**Management - Achieve Management
Excellence & World Class Leadership Skills In
7 Simple Steps**

**Sales - Easily Sell Anything To Anyone &
Achieve Sales Excellence In 7 Simple Steps**